NATIONAL GEOGRAPHIC

Ladders

WELCOME TO CHINA

AROUND THE WORLD

WELCOME TO CHINA!

by Cynthia Clampitt

> Imagine trying to find a friend on this street! Shoppers clog the shopping district in Shanghai, China.

SAY IT IN CHINESE!

qíng (ching) means "please"

xìexìe (shyeh-shyeh) means "thank you"

Ní hǎo mā? (NEE how mah) means "How are you?"

ON THE MOVE

Do you know how much one billion is? If you counted to one billion, it would take more than 30 years. The number of people living in China, or China's **population**, is nearly one and one-half billion. That's a lot of people! China has the largest population of any country in the world.

Where do so many Chinese people live? Like people in the United States, the people of China live in different kinds of communities. For many years, most Chinese people lived in **villages**. A village is a kind of community. It is smaller than a city and is usually located in the country. In Chinese villages, many people work as farmers.

Recently, many village people have moved to China's huge cities. In cities, many people work in factories or offices instead of on farms. Cities in China are very busy. Shanghai (shang-HI) and Beijing (bay-JING), two of the largest cities in the world, are often crowded with people. Everywhere in China, people are always on the move!

Wó hén hăo. (WUH hen how) means "I'm very well."

wŏ jìao (WUH jee-ow) means "my name is"

zài jìan (zai jee-en) means "good-bye"

A BUSY VILLAGE LIFE

Chinese villages are smaller and less crowded than cities. But the people who live in villages are still very busy. Some people in villages work as teachers in schools and doctors in hospitals. But most villagers are farmers. Chinese farmers have to grow a lot of food to feed their country's huge population and to feed their own families.

Many Chinese farmers grow rice or wheat. These crops grow well in China. They can be used to make many different foods. Children help on their family's farm by taking care of farm animals, such as sheep and goats. They gather firewood so the family can cook their meals. Children also pick fruit from fruit trees and sell it in nearby markets.

There is always time to have fun after farm chores are done. Children race each other to the village markets. They float down rivers on flat rafts and take bike rides on country roads.

> Children who live in Chinese villages are very busy. They work on farms, do homework, and play with their friends.

∧ In China, families like to eat together. This family eats food that has been grown on farms in their village.

∧ Many village children help their families with farm work. They work before and after school.

∧ Ducks are common farm animals in Chinese villages. Families eat their eggs. They sell the extras at the village market.

LIFE AMONG *TALL BUILDINGS*

Almost half of China's population still lives in villages. But Chinese cities are growing every day. Cities such as Shanghai and Beijing have millions of people living in them. Chinese cities are exciting places. At every hour of the day and night, people work, study, and have fun.

In most Chinese cities, families live in small apartments in tall, narrow buildings. These types of buildings take up less land but have space for more people than short, wide buildings. In crowded cities, tall buildings are important because they are a place where large numbers of people can live in a small amount of space.

> Most city families don't have yards. Kids play in parks where there is plenty of space.

The streets in Chinese cities are packed with people walking, riding bicycles, and driving cars. Some people ride crowded trains and buses. Bright signs flash, and buses and taxis honk at people crossing the streets. Chinese cities are very busy places.

∧ Trains in Chinese cities fill up quickly with many people.

∧ These tall apartment buildings are in the Chinese city of Shanghai.

∧ In Chinese cities, even bikes can get stuck in traffic jams.

Check In What do children do for fun in China?

∧ Most rice paddies in China are built by hand. Some paddies have been used to grow rice for over 1,000 years.

THE UNDERWATER CROP

Rice is nice! In China, rice is the most important part of each meal. Rice is a small white or brown grain that comes from a plant. Rice plants grow well in warm and wet places such as southern China.

Farmers have grown rice in China for thousands of years. In the spring, farmers plow their land. Then they plant seeds in paddies. A **paddy** is an area of land that is flooded with about six inches of water. Many paddies look like stair steps. Water flows from a higher paddy down into a lower one. Most crops do not grow well on flooded land, but rice does.

In the summer, farmers drain the water from the paddies. They pull out any weeds they see. Then they flood the fields again so the rice can keep growing. In autumn, they drain the paddies again. Then the farmers **harvest**, or gather, the rice crop. The rice is dried. Then it is taken to the mill. A mill is a building where the farmer gets the rice ready to take to the market.

by Becky Manfredini

RICE FOR SALE

Each rice grain has a dry outer shell that cannot be eaten. It is called the husk. At the mill, workers and machines remove the husks. Then the rice is cleaned to take out stones and dirt. No one wants to eat rice with stones in it! After it is cleaned, the rice is safe to eat.

The clean rice is poured into bags. The bags are put into boxes. Rice is grown in the country so it has to be sent to cities. Many city families buy rice in outdoor markets or in stores.

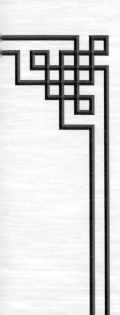

People sell rice in outdoor markets such as this one. Smart shoppers carry their rice home in a cart. Bags of rice are very heavy!

People have eaten rice for more than 5,000 years.

NOT JUST FOR EATING

Long ago, sticky rice was used as glue to hold walls and buildings together. Today, rice glue is used in many different ways, as shown below.

Need to write something down? For more than 1,000 years, Chinese people have been using rice to make paper. The surface of rice paper is smooth and white.

Chinese artists make little dolls out of rice powder and paper. People can buy these dolls in many of the outdoor markets.

11

RICE FOR BREAKFAST, LUNCH, AND DINNER

The Chinese word *fan* means "rice." It also means "meal." Rice is served at every meal in China. You might think that the Chinese would get tired of eating so much rice. They don't. Eating rice in China is not boring.

Rice is served in many ways. For breakfast, you might have a bowl of rice porridge with cinnamon. Porridge is a soft food

made from rice cooked in milk. For lunch, you might have soup with rice as well as steamed sticky rice with vegetables. For dinner, you might have vegetables and chicken with rice. At every meal, you eat with chopsticks instead of a fork. **Chopsticks** are thin sticks used to pick up and eat food.

In China, rice can always be found on the dinner table. It's delicious by itself, or eaten with another dish.

HOW TO HOLD AND USE CHOPSTICKS

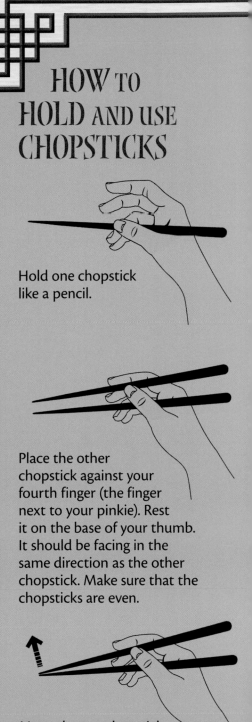

Hold one chopstick like a pencil.

Place the other chopstick against your fourth finger (the finger next to your pinkie). Rest it on the base of your thumb. It should be facing in the same direction as the other chopstick. Make sure that the chopsticks are even.

Move the top chopstick up and down. Hold the bottom chopstick still. Pinch a piece of stir-fried shrimp between the tips. Carefully bring the shrimp to your mouth. Mmm, mmm, good!

13

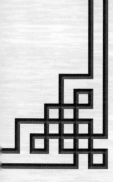

CELEBRATING with RICE

Chinese people celebrate holidays in many fun ways. They always cook and serve delicious foods made with rice.

Chinese New Year is a holiday that happens in January and February. It lasts for 15 days. People in China celebrate each new year by watching colorful fireworks, wearing bright clothing, and marching in parades. Chinese New Year is also a time for families to share special meals. Many people make sticky rice cakes. These sweet treats are said to bring good luck and a sweet life in the new year.

The last event during Chinese New Year is the Lantern Festival. People hang lanterns in their homes and shops. The lanterns are different colors, shapes, and sizes. Dancers perform with a big, colorful dragon that is a symbol of good luck. People make and eat sticky rice balls filled with nuts and fruits. The rice balls stand for family unity, or togetherness.

In both villages and cities, rice is a part of Chinese people's lives. Who would have thought that a little grain could be so important?

Colorful dragon dancers carry a cloth dragon on poles. The lead dancer moves the head. The rest of the dancers move the long body.

Check In   How do the people of China use rice in different ways?

The Thief and the Elephant

retold by Elizabeth Massie
illustrated by Rich Lo

Stories are an important part of a country's culture. They are meant to entertain us, but they can also teach us important lessons. A folk tale is a story passed down by families for many years. This Chinese folk tale teaches that honest people do not need to fear the truth.

Long ago in China, elephants were taught to do many things. They helped farmers plow their land, they helped build roads, and they helped woodcutters carry heavy logs. Many people believed elephants were as wise as they were strong. It was said that an elephant could see into a person's heart and know if he or she was lying or telling the truth.

One day, a woman visited a judge named Ko-Kia-Yong. She was very upset. "I have been robbed!" she said. "A man came into my house last night. He stole my bracelets and necklaces. I want the guilty man found and punished." She described the thief to the judge.

Ko-Kia-Yong told her he would do all he could to solve this crime. He sent out his officers to find five men who matched the description the woman had given. The five men were brought to court.

All five men were about the same height. Their hair was cut and combed in the same way. When the woman who had been robbed came into the courtroom, she looked at each man carefully. Then she pointed to one man and said that he was the thief.

"Are you sure he is the thief?" asked Ko-Kia-Yong.

The woman said, "Oh, yes, I am quite certain. I saw him run out of my house!"

The judge then opened a large door and brought in an elephant. "This is my elephant. She can tell what is in a person's mind and heart. She will find out who is innocent and who is guilty."

Four of the men stood smiling as the elephant touched their heads and chests with her trunk. The fifth man, however, trembled in fear. His face became red with worry. He was not the man the woman had accused of the robbery.

The judge watched as the elephant studied each man. Then he shouted, "Do your duty!" The elephant wrapped her trunk around the trembling man and handed him over to the officers. The man was taken to jail, where he confessed to the crime.

The woman was shocked. "I was sure I was right," she said.

Ko-Kia-Yong said, "In the future you must be careful whom you accuse."

The woman nodded and replied, "I will, sir."

Ko-Kia-Yong patted his elephant and said, "You have helped me judge wisely. Go now. Good food awaits you in your stable."

The elephant went back out through the large door, swinging her mighty trunk and waving her huge ears. The woman bowed to the judge and left the courtroom.

The next day, three wise men came to the courtroom to talk to the judge. They had many questions they wanted him to answer.

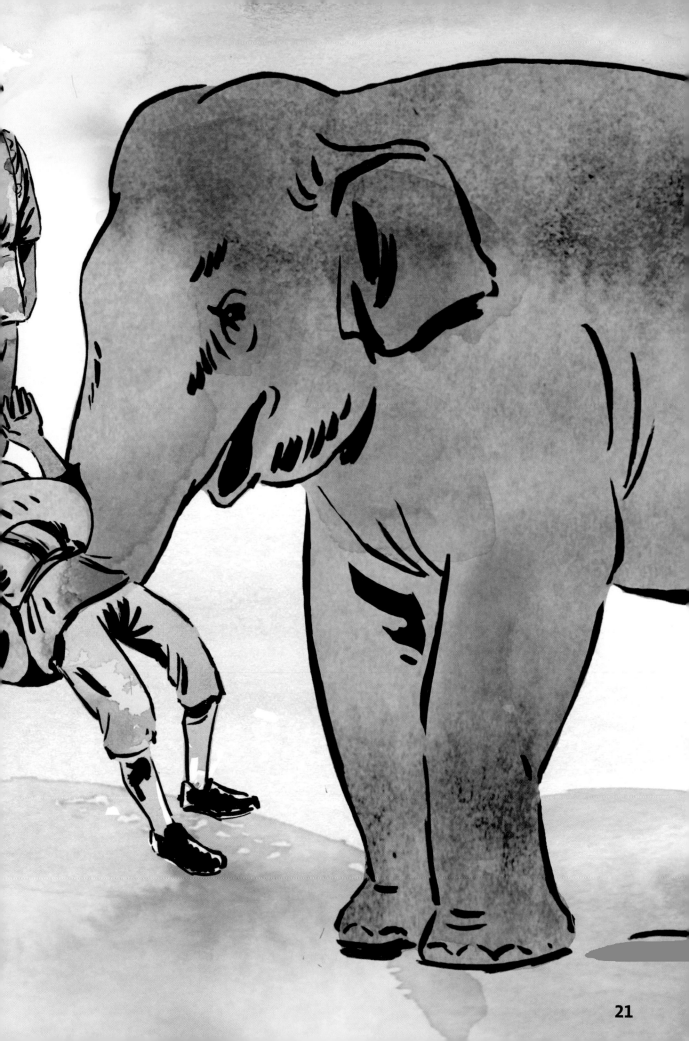

"We have heard about your elephant," said one wise man, "and we are amazed. We cannot believe that an animal can know the heart and mind of a man."

"Yes," agreed another wise man, "she picked the thief out. How did she do it? What do you feed your elephant? What tricks have you taught her?"

Ko-Kia-Yong just laughed and said, "My elephant eats what all elephants eat, and I have taught her no tricks."

The wise men were still confused. The judge continued, "Many people believe elephants have special powers. The five men who were brought in yesterday believed it. Because of their belief, the honest men were not worried. They knew they were innocent. But the thief was very afraid. He was sure the elephant would discover his crime."

"Ah," said the third wise man. "He could not hide his terror from the court."

"Yes," said Ko-Kia-Yong, "and by showing his guilt and fear, he showed that he was the thief."

The three wise men left the courtroom that day grateful to be honest men. They knew that living is much easier when you have no fear of the truth.

Check In Why was the guilty man scared of the elephant?

Discuss

1. What do you think connects the three selections that you read in this book? What makes you think that?

2. How is the life of a child who lives in a Chinese village different from that of a child who lives in the city?

3. How is rice an important part of Chinese celebrations?

4. Do you think you would have been able to pick out the guilty man in the folk tale? Why or why not?

5. What do you still wonder about life in China? How can you learn more?